Visiting the *Past*

Valley of the Kings

Rob Alcraft

Heinemann Library
Chicago, Illinois

Customer Service 888-454-2279

Designed by Visual Image
Illustrations by Visual Image
Printed in Hong Kong

04 03 02 01 00
10 9 8 7 6 5 4 3 2 1

Library of Congress Cataloging-in-Publication Data
Alcraft, Rob, 1966-
    Valley of the Kings / Rob Alcraft.
        p. cm. – (Visiting the past)
    Includes bibliographical references and index.
    Summary: Describes the hieroglyphics, tombs, tomb robbers, and
evidence of the past associated with the Valley of the Kings,
discussing the family life, land, work, culture, and warfare of the
ancient Egyptians.
    ISBN 1-57572-860-5 (library binding)
    1. Valley of the Kings (Egypt) Juvenile literature. 2. Egypt-
-Civilization—to 332 B.C. Juvenile literature. [1. Valley of the
Kings (Egypt) 2. Egypt—Antiquities. 3. Egypt—Civilization—To
332 B.C.] I. Title. II. Series.
DT73.B44A54 1999
932—dc21   99-11040
                                                CIP

Acknowledgments
The publishers would like to thank Phil Cook and Magnet Harlequin for permission to
reproduce all photographs, with the exception of those on pages 12, 13, 15, and 20,
reproduced with permission of the Ashmolean Museum, Oxford, England.

Cover photograph reproduced with permission of Erich Lessing, AKG London.

The author would like to thank Phil Cook for the photographs and Mubarak Ali Hasan Meki
for the fixing.

Every effort has been made to contact copyright holders of any material reproduced in this
book. Any omissions will be rectified in subsequent printings if notice is given to the
Publisher.

Some words are shown in bold, **like this.** You can find out what they mean
by looking in the glossary.

Contents

Egypt and the Valley of the Kings

Egypt is a desert country, but it is dominated by one river, the Nile River. Where the Nile cuts through the desert the land is lush and green. Water for growing crops trickles in ditches, and palm trees grow.

For over 1,700 years, between about 2700 and 1000 B.C., Egypt was one of the world's great civilizations. Protected from enemies by the natural barrier of the desert, ancient Egypt grew rich and powerful. Kings—called pharaohs— ruled, and were regarded as living gods.

Between 1550 and 1075 B.C., during a period we call the New Kingdom, the pharaohs made their capital at Thebes. They built temples and monuments. On the west bank of the Nile, a rocky, desert valley was chosen as the burial place of the pharaohs. This is the Valley of the Kings.

This is the burial chamber of the Pharaoh Ramses VI. His is one of 62 tombs carved into the rock of the Valley of the Kings.

In the time of the pharaohs, Egypt would have looked very much like this. Archaeologists think that the band of green fields beside the Nile River may have reached farther into the desert. Wild animals, including leopards and hyenas, would have roamed the edges of the desert.

The Valley of the Kings

The tombs in the Valley of the Kings tell a story more than 3,000 years old. On the walls of the tombs are pictures and writings that tell of the pharaohs buried inside them and the civilization over which they ruled.

The ancient Egyptians saw the tombs as magical places. They believed that the tomb protected the dead pharaoh's body for the journey to the **Underworld**. The pharaohs were buried with possessions such as clothes and fabulous, golden treasures they would need in life after death. They were also buried with books of magic to raise them from the dead.

Archaeologists have found and explored many tombs in the Valley of the Kings and in the hills nearby. They have translated writings, both on **papyrus** and carved in stone, that were found in the tombs and the great temples built by the pharaohs. Ruins have even been uncovered of the village where the workers who built the tombs once lived. These things tell us the story of life in the time of the pharaohs.

These giant statues, called the **Colossi** of Memnon, are 3,350 years old. They are all that survives of a massive temple built by the Pharaoh Amenhotep III.

These symbols are **hieroglyphs**. For a long time, no one knew how to read hieroglyphs. But in 1799, a French soldier found what is now called the Rosetta Stone. The stone had an

inscription. It was written three times, in three different languages. One of the inscriptions was in ancient Greek, which was still understood. Another was in the mysterious hieroglyphs. The Greek made it possible to translate and read hieroglyphs. The third version was an informal Egyptian script. The stone is now in the British Museum in London, England.

5

Pharaohs, Temples, and Gods

Near the Valley of the Kings, there are ruins of more than fifteen great temples, built on the orders of the New Kingdom pharaohs. These temples show just how powerful the pharaohs were. The buildings would have needed workers, slaves, and building materials from all over Egypt. They would have taken years to finish.

The temple walls that remain are covered in pictures and **hieroglyphs** that praise the bravery and skill of the pharaohs. They also show the gods of the ancient Egyptians.

The ancient Egyptians believed in many gods. The most powerful god at the time of the New Kingdom was Amon-Re, the god of the sun. Then there was the goddess Isis, who gave life to the dead. The ancient Egyptians even believed that the pharaoh was a god, living on earth. He served the other gods. His service guaranteed life for Egypt—from the rising of the sun to the yearly flood that watered the fields and enabled the Egyptian farmers to grow food.

This is Re, sometimes called Amon-Re or Ra, the god of the sun. He was thought to have traveled across the sky with the sun, giving life to the world.

The ancient temples were painted in bright colors. When temples were buried under sand and rubble, the colors were protected from the sun and wind. They still look bright, 3,000 years later.

The temple of Hatshepsut

One of the most beautiful temples that survives today is the temple of Queen Hatshepsut, who ruled Egypt from about 1479 to 1457 B.C. It stands on the east bank of the Nile, across the river from the ancient city of Thebes, now called Luxor.

There are many stories on the walls of Hatshepsut's temple. One is of a journey to a land called Punt, which is the modern-day African country of Eritrea. The Queen sent boats to trade with the kings of Punt. Hieroglyphs on the walls tell the story. "The boats were loaded with large quantities of the wonders of Punt, with **myrrh** and living myrrh trees, with ebony wood and pure ivory, with incense, with baboons, monkeys, and dogs, with the skins of panthers from the South, with the natives and their sons. . . ."

The god Osiris was always painted wrapped like a mummy. The ancient Egyptians believed that Osiris had been murdered by his evil brother, Seth. Seth hacked up the body of Osiris and scattered the pieces along the Nile. But Isis, the wife of Osiris, searched for the pieces of the body and gathered them up. She wrapped them and brought Osiris back to life. He rose from the dead to become the god of the **Underworld**.

This is the temple of Hatshepsut. There are no pictures of Hatshepsut or hieroglyphs about her on the temple They were removed on the order of her nephew Thutmose III. He was angry that he had had to wait until Hatshepsut's death before he became pharaoh.

Journey into the Underworld

There were 62 tombs dug into the rock of the Valley of the Kings. Many hundreds more were dug for noblemen and craftsmen in the hills nearby. We know from the paintings and writings in these tombs that the ancient Egyptians believed that the tomb would keep their bodies safe. This would leave their spirits free to make the journey to the **Underworld** and eternal life.

The body was thought to be so important that it was mummified, so that it would keep forever in the safety of the tomb. Mummifying a body could take three months. First, the brain was pulled out through the nose. Then the dead person's lungs, liver, stomach, and intestines were removed and placed in special jars. The body was then dried in **natron**, rubbed with oil, and wrapped in long strips of **linen**. A picture of the dead person was painted on the coffin, so that the spirit could find the right body in the Underworld.

The mummy of the Pharaoh Tutankhamen, who died in 1323 B.C., still lies in his tomb in the Valley of the Kings. The only organ left inside his body is his heart. The heart, thought to be the most precious part of a person, was put back into the body during **embalming.**

This picture of the goddess Nut was painted on the ceiling of a tomb.

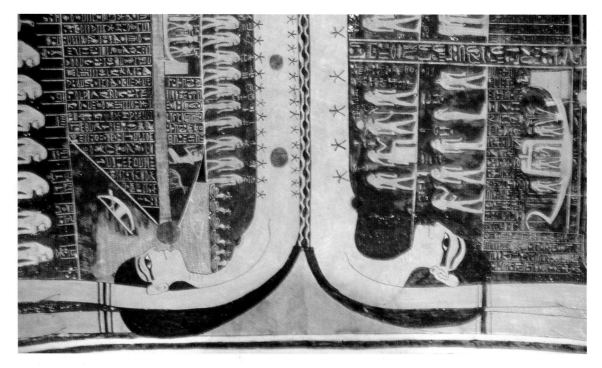

Judgment of the dead

Before the mummified body went into the tomb, there was a last ritual called the Opening of the Mouth. We know from paintings and **papyri** found in tombs that priests dressed as gods would touch the mouth of the mummy. This was believed to give back to the dead person the power of speech and the ability to eat and drink.

Then the body was placed in the tomb. This was when the judgment of the dead began. The ancient Egyptians believed that this would be a time of terror and danger. The dead had to be well prepared for the difficult journey. With them in the tomb were placed the magic and spells they would need to get through the trials ahead.

The spirit of the dead person would be judged against 42 crimes, which included murder and stealing. Then the heart would be weighed against a feather to see if it was innocent. A person who passed these tests would enter the Underworld and live with the god Osiris. If the heart was weighed down by sin, the person would be devoured by a monster and the soul, or spirit, would die.

Anubis was the **jackal**-headed god of embalming. This carving is on the wall of Hatshepsut's temple.

The Egyptians believed that many dangers faced them on the journey to the Underworld. The dead had spells written on their tombs and on papyrus to help them on this dangerous

journey. The spells tell us a lot about what the Egyptians thought goodness was. This is part of one spell: "Behold I have come to you; I have brought you truth. I have not done falsehood; I have not robbed; I have not taken food; I have not stolen bread; I have not deprived the orphan of his property; I have not made terror; I have not been hot tempered . . . I am pure."

Tomb Robbers

In 1881, a secret tomb was discovered, just beyond the Valley of the Kings. It was cut into bare rock. It had none of the paintings or treasure of other tombs. Instead, piled up inside, were the coffins and bodies of some of the greatest pharaohs of ancient Egypt.

Labels on the mummies told how they had been moved from the Valley of the Kings, in secret, in 960 B.C. Robbers were looting tombs in the Valley, and priests brought the mummies to this plain tomb to keep them safe.

We can tell from this event that the pharaohs found it impossible to guard the old burial sites. We know from the number of empty tombs that the robbers must have been very determined, and often successful.

The Valley of the Kings was used as a burial place by the pharaohs for more than 500 years. The riches buried here were always a target for robbers.

Robbers and execution

The penalty for tomb robbing was death. Yet the robbers still came, drawn by the huge treasures that had been buried with the pharaohs.

One robber who was caught was called Amunpnufer. His torture, confession, and trial were recorded by a **scribe** on a **papyrus**, now kept at the British Museum in London. "He was examined by beating with the stick. His hands and feet were twisted. He said: '. . .we broke open the tombs . . . and brought away their inner coffins that were in them. We stripped off the gold and silver which was upon them and stole it.'" Amunpnufer, having confessed, was executed. Other trial records tell us that execution usually meant being **impaled** on a stake.

The giant, granite coffin of Ramses VI lies in pieces on the floor of his burial chamber. More than 3,000 years ago, robbers broke into this tomb. They broke open the coffin by lighting fires on it to make it crack. They wanted to get at the mummy, which would have been covered in gold.

This is the passage that leads down to the tomb of Pharaoh Ramses VI. Tombs like this one were sealed with stone slabs and were also guarded. But the robbers got in eventually.

The Tomb of Tutankhamen

Early in the twentieth century, **archaeologists** began a careful search of the Valley of the Kings. They believed there might be some tombs that had not been discovered by robbers.

One man who searched the Valley was Howard Carter. He employed hundreds of Egyptians to dig and move tons of rock. He worked for years. Then, in 1922, one of the workers found a step, then a sealed doorway. It led into the tomb of Tutankhamen.

It took Carter nearly ten years to study and remove all the 3,500 objects inside Tutankhamen's tomb. It was a fabulous treasure—a time capsule of objects from the everyday life of a king. Tutankhamen even had his sandals buried with him. They are made of wood, which was very rare and expensive in Egypt. Probably very uncomfortable, they show that the Pharaoh never had to walk far! He probably usually traveled in a chair carried by servants.

Tutankhamen was just nine years old when he became Pharaoh. He ruled for nine years and died in 1323 B.C.

12

The glint of gold

Carter broke into the tomb. Holding up a lighted candle, he peered into the darkness of the first chamber. He saw a jumble of furniture and objects. Gold glinted from the shadows. There were statues of gods, model boats, tables, beds, chairs, boxes, and even a chariot. Everything that Tutankhamen would have needed on his journey to the **Underworld** was here. There was food, drink, and the books of magic and spells that would help the Pharaoh as he faced judgment.

Beyond this first chamber stood a second doorway, guarded by two statues of Tutankhamen. Breaking through this door, Carter discovered a wall of gold. It was the first of four **shrines** enclosing the coffin and body of the Pharaoh. In the fourth shrine lay a stone coffin. Inside that were three more coffins. The last was covered in gold.

Robbers had broken into Tutankhamen's tomb twice. Both times the robbers were discovered before they could loot the coffin chamber. The fact that the tomb had been disturbed probably explains why it was so messy when Carter found it.

War and Weapons

The Egyptians of the New Kingdom had an organized and deadly army. Ramses III, who ruled from 1187 to 1156 B.C., ordered a great temple to be built. Pictures in the temple boast about his army's victories and his own bravery. Carvings on the walls, which are 66 feet (20 meters) high, show him sacrificing his enemies to the gods.

The temple has a high gate tower. It was surrounded by a massive wall of mud brick. Inside was a palace with a sacred lake. During important festivals, the Pharaoh would come to the temple and stand at a high window. It would seem as if he was appearing by magic—looking just as great and mysterious as a living god was expected to look.

This is the temple of Ramses III. It was one of more than fifteen great temples built on the west bank of the Nile, below the Valley of the Kings.

This carving shows Ramses III in his chariot, crushing his enemies.

The Sea Peoples

One of the great battles celebrated by the temple is the victory over the Sea Peoples in 1174 B.C. The Sea Peoples came from the islands of the Mediterranean. Ramses III and his soldiers fought them in fast war boats. Anyone who was left alive after the battle was either taken as a slave or slaughtered. The temple wall shows a mound of severed hands and other body parts, hacked off by soldiers as a record of their victories.

The army used chariots and **infantry**. Models in tombs show the infantry marching with spears and leather shields. Archers would go in front to kill and frighten the enemy by raining arrows from the sky. Their bows have been found in tombs, and we know they had a range of about 650 feet (200 meters). Bodies found in a mass burial of soldiers had arrowheads stuck in their bones.

Soldiers had to endure danger and hardship. They also had to help build the temples and monuments of the pharaohs. But they got a share of whatever they could plunder from their enemies. This is the story of one soldier, who fought on a war boat like this tomb model: "I am the chief of sailors, Ahmose, son of Abana. . . . I was presented with the gold of honor (a medal) seven times in front of the whole land. I was given male and female slaves, and given many fields. I served as an officer, on the ship *Offering*, while I was still a youth. Then I was transferred … because of my bravery. I followed the King on foot when he rode in his chariot and, when he attacked the city of Avaris, I showed such bravery before His Majesty that I was promoted to the ship *Shining in Memphis*."

The Eyes and Ears of the Pharaoh

Many times in Egypt's history, pharaohs were murdered. Ancient letters and stories from the Old Kingdom, which flourished between about 2575 and 2130 B.C., warn the pharaohs to beware. "Trust no one," they say, "not even a brother or a friend." But pharaohs could not rule alone. They had to have advisers.

The man the pharaoh trusted most was the **vizier,** or prime minister. He was the most powerful man in Egypt after the pharaoh. Sometimes viziers even called themselves the "eyes and ears of the pharaoh." Around 1425 B.C., a man called Rekhmire was vizier.

This door opens into Rekhmire's burial chamber.

Rekhmire's tomb was found empty. Experts think he might have been buried in the Valley of the Kings as a reward for his service to two pharaohs. Although his body has never been found, this portrait of him is in his tomb. Rekhmire would have believed that if his body was destroyed, this picture would act as a substitute body for his journey into the **Underworld.** In his picture, he is facing a false door at the end of his tomb. Through the door is the Underworld.

The tomb of a vizier

Rekhmire served two pharaohs, Thutmose III and Amenhotep II. We know from the beauty and size of his tomb near the Valley of the Kings that he was rich and powerful. Paintings show that he had a wife and three sons.

Rekhmire's tomb, like the pharaohs' tombs, contains the magic symbols that would send the dead man to the Underworld. The tomb gives a record of Rekhmire's life. It is also a description of his job.

Rekhmire was in charge of the pharaoh's **granary** and the **treasury**. Paintings in the tomb show that he controlled the building work on many temples. He visited **estates** and controlled the collection of taxes. The loot from battles and conquered enemies came to Rekhmire first. He even acted for the pharaoh as supreme judge in Egypt. Perhaps most important of all, Rekhmire was in

Rekhmire was responsible for the workers who lived in the village of Deir el-Medina. They are shown here on the walls of his tomb.

charge of the police. Messages from all over Egypt came to Rekhmire, telling him news from forts and guard posts and reporting people who tried to avoid the forced labor that was required of everyone by the pharaoh.

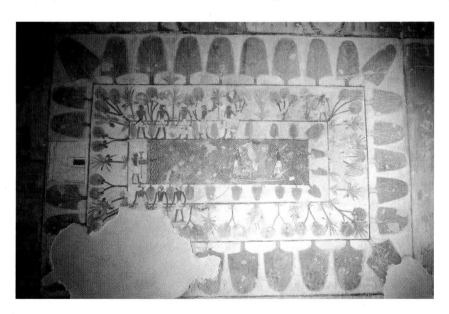

Rekhmire had this garden painted in his tomb so that he would be granted a garden as beautiful in the Underworld.

17

The Keepers of Words

Scribes were writers, accountants, engineers, and administrators. Scribes were very powerful in Egypt, largely because only they and priests were taught to write. They kept records and lists, calculated taxes, and paid wages. They wrote letters, which revealed personal and private details of the rich and powerful. It is because of the writings of scribes—such as those on the walls of tombs in the Valley of the Kings—that we know so much about the beliefs and lives of the ancient Egyptians.

It took seven years to become a scribe. School was a temple courtyard. A rich student might have a home tutor. Student scribes learned by copying texts. Many texts were composed by teachers to give sharp warnings. The scribe Amenemope wrote in one copy text, "Pass no day in idleness or you will be beaten. The ear of a boy is on his back. He listens when he is beaten."

This painting in Rekhmire's tomb shows a scribe weighing and recording gold and silver. Scribes were everywhere in ancient Egypt. They checked, listed, and kept account of harvests and building projects. They looked down on other jobs. The scribe Khaty wrote in one copy lesson, "I have seen the metal worker at the mouth of his furnace, his fingers like the stuff of crocodile, he stinks more than fish **roe**. . . . The gardener is bringing a **yoke**, each of his shoulders weighted with age and a great swelling on his neck which is festering."

Magical words

Scribes used writing called **hieratic** for everyday work. Hieratic writing ran from right to left and could be written quickly. But the Egyptians also had a sacred form of writing. This writing used **hieroglyphs**.

For the Egyptians, hieroglyphs were a kind of magic. They believed that things could be created simply by writing their names. If it was written in their tomb that someone owned land and gold, then it became true. It would actually happen. They were so powerful that, at times, some hieroglyphs such as the "horned viper"—the sign for the letter *F*—were written in bits. With the viper in bits, it could not come to life and slither off the wall to bite someone.

Hieroglyphs do not use letters like English. They consist of pictures and signs. Some are signs for sounds, some for names. There are over 700 different hieroglyphs. Not all hieroglyphs are carved on stone. Scribes also wrote on **papyrus**, a kind of paper made from reeds. Rolls of papyri were often buried in tombs. Papyrus was very long-lasting. It could even be scrubbed clean if a scribe wanted to reuse it.

The Tomb Builders

Close to the Valley of the Kings, there are the ruins of a village. This is where the men who built the tombs and temples of the pharaohs lived. They were skilled craftsmen. They included **masons**, artists, **draftsmen**, **scribes,** and builders.

Their village was called Deir el-Medina. The ruins show 120 houses packed into a small space. Deir el-Medina was a bustling place. The narrow main street would have been choked with traders, servants, and animals. Customers from shops, bars, and workshops would have spilled out into the street.

This is a model house from a tomb. Egyptian houses would have looked much like this.

Working, shirking, and going on strike

We know from scribes' records found at the village that the craftsmen worked in two gangs, one for each side of a tomb. An Egyptian week lasted ten days. The men worked for eight days, then had two days off.

They were organized and could work quickly. Stone cutters, using simple mallets and chisels, would carve tunnels and rooms into the rock. Next came the plasterers, then the teams of draftsmen and artists, who would sketch the designs and **hieroglyphs**. Next, mistakes would be corrected and the designs inked in. Then they would be colored.

But the workers also **shirked** as much as they could. From the records kept by scribes, we know that work days were lost for brewing beer, building houses, and drinking. Workers also had a lot of religious holidays. We know from scribes that the workers of Deir el-Medina staged the world's first recorded strike, in 1157 B.C. Their pay had not appeared, so they camped out near the Valley of the Kings, at the temple of Horemheb, complaining, "We have no clothing, no fat, no fish, no vegetables."

Houses were built on stone foundations. They were of mud brick, with plastered walls, flat roofs, and vents to catch cooling breezes. Most of the workers in Deir el-Medina would have had maids and servants who would cook and carry for their wives.

These metal workers (left), shown in a painting from Rekhmire's tomb, were highly skilled. Records kept by scribes show that they were also well paid. Egypt did not use money, so the men were paid in grain, beer, water, fish, vegetables, wood, pottery, and clothing. On festival days, there were bonuses of oil, salt, wine, and meat.

Family Life

Families were important to the Egyptians. People building tombs would have pictures of their children and servants painted on the walls. They wanted their whole family with them in the **Underworld**.

Scribes gave plenty of advice to young people about families. This advice still exists and gives us a good idea of what the Egyptians thought about marriage and children. A scribe called Any wrote, "Take a wife while you are still young, so that she may bear a son for you. Happy is the man whose family is numerous, he is respected on account of his children."

The villagers of Deir el-Medina built tombs and chapels for themselves and their families. They believed their **ancestors** would keep them safe, so they would leave gifts of beer and grain to feed these ancestors in the Underworld.

Marriage

Families arranged marriages for their children. The marriage ceremony was often just moving home, as the girl went from her father's house to her new husband's. The wedding gifts would follow in a big procession.

Girls were married at about thirteen years old. It seems young, but studies of mummies and human remains from ancient Egypt show that most people did not live past the age of 36. Childbirth was so dangerous that many women died even earlier. Only the very rich lived longer, because their lives and food were better. Pharaoh Ramses II was over 70 years old when he died.

But women did have rights—more than in many countries today. There were marriage contracts, which meant that they got some property if there was a divorce. They were also allowed to inherit and own property.

Cats were sacred to the Egyptians. Sometimes they were mummified, like this one from a museum in Egypt. Cat mummies were sold to temple visitors as offerings. Live cats were kept to catch mice and to fetch birds killed by hunters in the marshes.

Egyptian houses were painted beautiful colors, sometimes outside as well as in. This pattern is from the ceiling of a tomb. Its owner would have wanted a grand and beautiful house in the Underworld, and he believed that painting a beautiful ceiling would help get him one.

Beauty and Pleasure

Rich Egyptians loved wearing beautiful clothes and jewelry. Sometimes they would have their clothes buried with them. Kha was an architect who lived sometime around 1500 B.C. He had 50 **loincloths** and 26 shirts buried in his tomb near the Valley of the Kings.

Women's dresses were long and flowing, and both men and women wore as much jewelry as they could afford. They wore golden neck bands, bracelets, rings, and earrings. Because the Egyptians did not know how to dye clothes, they added color to their outfits with jewelry. Many pieces still survive. They are often beautiful, skillfully made from gold, glass, and stone.

Wigs were always fashionable. Because wigs needed complicated care, Egyptians had professional hairdressers, or skilled friends, to help them look their best.

Body hair, makeup, and smells

All sorts of mirrors, combs, tweezers, and makeup pots have been found in Egyptian tombs. Even the makeup itself is sometimes included. The Egyptians used lots of eye paint. It was sometimes colored green by copper ore or black by lead. They applied the paint in thick lines from the eyebrow to the base of the nose. They colored their palms and nails, and even the soles of their feet, with red **henna**.

The Egyptians also worried about personal **hygiene** and the way they looked. Body hair was thought of as ugly. People usually kept their hair short, and men would have their heads and faces shaved, usually by traveling barbers who used large copper razors. For those with special problems, there were **papyri** with medical advice. These gave prescriptions for making hair grow or to keep it from turning gray, and for removing unwanted body hair, wrinkles, and spots, as well as for dealing with problem smells.

Lipstick and eye makeup were used by both men and women.

Music and dance

Paintings on tomb walls show how important music was to the Egyptians. They loved parties and dancing, and made sure they included these in their lists of things to take to the **Underworld**. Though we don't know what the music sounded like, because it was never written down and is impossible to recreate, many musical instruments, like those in Tutankhamen's tomb, still survive.

We know from mummies that professional dancers and musicians like these would often have a little tattoo of Bes, the god of recreation, on their thigh for good luck. This scene is from a painting of Rekhmire's funeral, but musicians and dancers would be hired for all sorts of feasts and celebrations.

Land and Work

All the power and splendor of ancient Egypt was supported by the work of the poorest people. These were the farmers, peasants, and slaves. We know from paintings in tombs, and from records and accounts kept by **scribes**, that most of them owned nothing. If they farmed land, much of their harvest would go to the landowner to pay the rent.

What one scribe wrote about farming is probably not far from the truth. "The farmer laments more than the **guinea fowl**, his voice louder than the raven's, with his fingers made swollen and with an excessive stink."

This is a man called Sennefer and his wife. It is a tomb painting, so they are shown wearing their best clothes in the hope that they would have such clothes in the **Underworld.** The wheat is also much taller than it would have been, but the picture shows how the Egyptians used oxen and wooden plows.

Forced labor

Worst of all was the work peasants were expected to do during the Nile flood. The flood began in July and soon covered the fields, making farming impossible. So the pharaoh made the peasants do other jobs.

The first job was digging the dikes, canals, and channels that held the flood waters and watered the fields. Then there was building work. Peasants would drag huge stones across the desert and build the walls and columns of the great monuments. They worked in the heat of summer, when the temperature could rise above 104°F (40°C).

Working in such heat was so unpleasant that anyone rich enough paid other people to do it for them. Or if they couldn't face it, they would run away. There are many trial records of people trying to avoid forced labor. If they were caught, they would be enslaved for life. If they escaped, their families would be enslaved instead.

The shaduf, or water lifter, is still sometimes used in Egypt. For the ancient Egyptians, it was an essential way of lifting water from ditches and canals into the fields.

Writings on tomb walls tell us that the Egyptians also believed that the gods would make them do work in the Underworld. They did everything they could to avoid the possibility. They would have little figures called shabtis made for their tombs. The figures would act as servants and slaves in the next life. When the dead people were called upon to work, they would call the shabtis, which would do the work for them.

There were very few kinds of trees that grew in ancient Egypt. But farmers grew grapes and made wine, which was a great luxury.

Timeline

c.3000 B.C.	King Namur unites upper and lower Egypt and establishes his capital at Memphis.
c.2575–c.2130 B.C.	The period called the Old Kingdom. Pyramids, including the Great Pyramid at Giza, are built as tombs for pharaohs.
c.2130–1938 B.C.	First intermediate period. No pharaoh is able to take effective control of Egypt, leaving Egypt in chaos during this period.
2008–1957 B.C.	Mentuhotep I moves Egypt's capital to Thebes.
1938–c.1600 B.C.	Middle Kingdom. Strong pharaohs regain power. Osiris, god of the **Underworld**, is worshiped widely.
c.1600–1550 B.C.	Second intermediate period
1550–1075 B.C.	New Kingdom
1504–1492 B.C.	Reign of Thutmose I, the first pharaoh to be buried in the Valley of the Kings.
1479–1457 B.C.	Queen Hatshepsut rules Egypt as **regent** for Thutmose III.
1479–1425 B.C.	Reign of Thutmose III. Many of his high officials, including Rekhmire, build tombs around Thebes.
1427–1400 B.C.	Reign of Amenhotep II. He first served as joint ruler with his father Thutmose III and then on his own.
1390–1353 B.C.	Reign of Amenhotep III, who constructed many huge buildings, including the **Colossi** of Memnon
1332–1323 B.C.	Reign of Tutankhamen. He was mostly notable for his intact tomb, which has given **archaeologists** a wealth of information about Egyptian life and beliefs.
1279–1213 B.C.	Reign of Ramses II
1187–1156 B.C.	Reign of Ramses III, who was victorious in a war with the Sea Peoples of the Mediterranean.
1145–1137 B.C.	Reign of Ramses VI
1075–664 B.C.	Third intermediate period
332 B.C.	Egypt invaded by Macedonians under Alexander the Great
A.D. 1799	The Rosetta Stone, which enabled scholars to understand **hieroglyphs**, is discovered by a French soldier.
A.D. 1922	Howard Carter discovers the tomb of Tutankhamen.

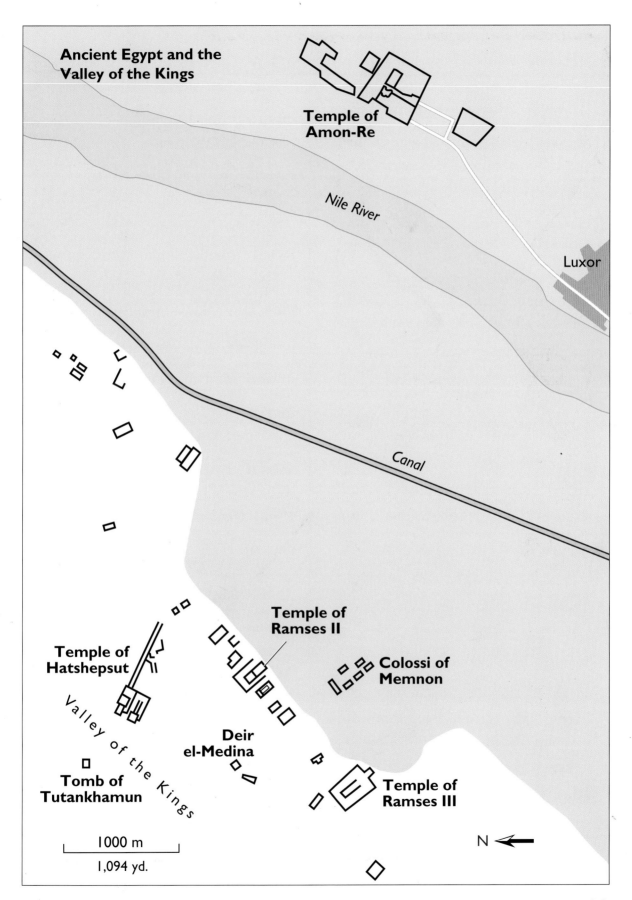

Ancient Egypt and the Valley of the Kings

Temple of
Amon-Re

Nile River

Luxor

Canal

Temple of
Ramses II

Temple of
Hatshepsut

Colossi of
Memnon

Valley of the Kings

Deir
el-Medina

Tomb of
Tutankhamun

Temple of
Ramses III

1000 m
1,094 yd.

N

Glossary

ancestor relative from whom you are descended and who can be traced through either of your parents

archaeologist someone who studies ancient cultures by looking at things people have left behind, such as buildings and pottery

Colossi plural of "Colossus," a huge statue

draftsman someone who draws detailed plans, such as for buildings

embalming process of preserving a dead body by treating it with chemicals

estate large area of land, containing homes and farms, all owned by one person

granary building where grain is stored

guinea fowl bird found in Africa. It has a loud, mournful cry.

henna red-orange dye made from the leaves of a shrub

hieratic simplified form of ancient Egyptian writing

hieroglyphs ancient Egyptian form of writing, in which pictures are used to represent sounds and words

hygiene cleanliness needed to keep healthy

impale to pierce something with a sharp point, such as a spear

infantry soldiers who fight on foot with light weapons

inscription something carved or written on an object such as a rock or coin

jackal wild dog found in Africa and Asia

linen cloth made from flax

loincloth cloth worn around the hips

mason someone who carves stone

myrrh sweet-smelling gum used to make perfume

natron mineral found in dried-up lakes, used by the ancient Egyptians for embalming

papyrus (The plural is **papyri**) material from an Egyptian plant that was used to write on

regent someone who rules in place of someone else, usually because the real ruler is too young

roe eggs of a female fish

scribe person who was trained in hieroglyphic writing

shirk to avoid something, especially work

shrine sacred or holy place

treasury either a place where money is kept or the department that controls what a country earns, borrows, lends, and spends

Underworld place where, the ancient Egyptians believed, a person's spirit went after death. It was ruled by the god Osiris.

vizier a very high-ranking official, especially a prime minister

yoke wooden bar fixed across the shoulders for carrying heavy loads

More Books to Read

Bendick, Jeanne. *Egyptian Tombs.* Danbury, Conn: Franklin Watts, Incorporated, 1989.

Chapman, Gillian *The Egyptians.* Des Plaines, Ill: Heinemann Library, 1998.

Clayton, Peter A. *The Valley of the Kings.* Austin, Tex: Raintree Steck-Vaughn, 1995.

Green, Robert. *Tutankhamun.* Franklin Watts, Incorporated, 1996.

Millard, Anne. *The Pyramids: The Latest Secrets Revealed in the Light of Recent Scientific Discoveries.* Brookfield, Conn: Millbrook Press, 1995.

Steele, Philip. *The Egyptians & the Valley of the Kings.* Parsippany, NJ: Silver Burdett Press, 1994.

Index